ISBN 978-0-692-93298-8

Cover design by Tracy Spencer

Printed in the United States of America

HEART TO HEART

Encouragement,
Advice and
Inspiration
For
Teen Girls

SHARON Y. JUDIE & FRIENDS

Acknowledgements

To God be the glory forever and ever! Amen. (Galatians 1:5)

First and foremost, I'd like to express my heartfelt gratitude to my husband, Carl, for believing in me. I thank God for how you lovingly support everything I set out to do. You inspire me to take the limits off and soar.

I give special thanks to my children, Dorisha Smith and Kyle Loud. I am proud of both of you and I am glad I was chosen to be your mom. Keep reaching for the stars!

I am so grateful that my parents are able to celebrate this accomplishment with me (O. L. Douglas, Sr., Doris J. Tipton, Yvonne M. Douglas, and Chester Tipton, Jr.). I'm an author! I give them kudos, because before the term *co-parenting* was popular, they had perfected it and ensured I had a great childhood. Thank you for loving me through my tumultuous teenage years and continuing to support me today as I walk in my purpose.

I have so much gratitude for my brothers and sister: Lee Douglas, Jerrod Douglas and Kenya Jones. Thank you for the special bond we have, the silly secrets that we share and for simply making life fun.

I'm grateful for the way we love and support one another.

I have some amazingly supportive friends who have been my personal cheerleading squad as they lovingly prayed for this project from the beginning and kept me accountable. I can't name every person, but I must give special thanks to Sheila Darling, Tina Rosado, Cyndy Gupton, Raelea Burkett, Tranette Sanders, Joyce Isles and Benita Thomas. I thank you for loving me, encouraging me and praying for and supporting every vision I've shared with you. You pushed, prayed and pulled me to the finish line.

A very special thanks to Candace Medina for reminding me that all things are possible and that I simply must believe in myself. Your encouragement was the spark that ignited the *Daddy's Girl* movement, including the *Daddy's Girl* stage play and the *Daddy's Girl Empowerment Summit.*

I give honorable mention to Pastor Ed Robinson, Author LaShane Moore, Robin Devonish, LaQuisha Mitchell, Kim Fomby Jefferson, and Dr. Beverly Crockett for their assistance, inspiration and motivation to complete this book.

I utter my unending gratitude to all those who have given their support in any way and to those who paved the way to make this book possible.

Finally, last, but by no means least, I offer a huge round of applause to the special heroes - the men who contributed letters to this project. You shared from your heart and I am eternally thankful. May God bless everything you do.

If you know your value and worth,
no one can devalue you

Dedication

I lovingly dedicate this book to every young lady (or woman) who has ever felt overlooked, undervalued or insignificant. May the contents of this book empower and encourage you and remind you of your worth.

And

My grandchildren
My love for you knows no boundaries

Foreword

As a father of three beautiful daughters, brother to seven inspirational sisters and the husband of a beautiful queen, I know and highly respect the value of women. It pains my heart to see and hear about the myriad of abuses, chaos and torment that our young girls and women face.

In my role as a pastor, I am both privileged and challenged by the stories that adult women and young girls share about feeling like they don't belong or not feeling accepted by others, especially by young men, as well as adult men.

I encourage these ladies to never forget who they are and to Whom they belong - queens and daughters of our Heavenly Father. To that end, I am highly convinced that someone needs to continue to engage these ladies and remind them of their value, vivaciousness and vitality.

That is what Sharon Y. Judie has done with *Heart to Heart: Encouragement, Advice and Inspiration for Teen Girls.* It is an awesome compilation of letters written to encourage young girls and offer loving advice to help navigate peacefully through the teen years. These practical, personal and powerful stories and letters will inspire you to keep pressing forward with courage. They are written by men who have your best interest at heart, because they have daughters and sisters that they love.

In Psalm 139:14, the Psalmist wrote, "I will praise thee; for I am fearfully and wonderfully made: marvelous are thy works; and that my soul knoweth right well." Your Heavenly Father made you to be special and one-of-a-kind, so give yourself permission to walk boldly. You are God's daughter and He loves you.

Pastor Ed Robinson
Hope in Christ Community Church
http://www.hopeunity.org

To My Daddy, O. L. Douglas, Sr.

Dear Daddy,

Although your memory isn't as sharp as it once was, I'm thankful that I still have mine. I reflect back on childhood memories of growing up, carefree and happy, without a care in the world. Every time I call you, I laugh to hear you retell stories from my childhood. These stories have withstood time – as you have been telling them since I was young. I have heard each story so many times that I can recite each story, word-for-word. But, I don't. I cherish the things that make you happy. Being a father has definitely been a source of happiness for you.

When I was growing up, you never missed a piano recital or track meet or any event that I invited you to attend. I was almost 30 years old when I joined a softball league sponsored by my employer. No matter how late at night my games were scheduled, I could always find your face in the crowd. Fortunately few balls came in my direction because I wasn't a good athlete, but, at the end of each game, you told me how proud you were of me.

I was 19 or 20 the day you got baptized. I cried tears of joy, knowing that when you died, you would spend eternity with Jesus and since that day 35+ years ago, you have shared the gospel with everyone who has crossed your path.

When you and my mother divorced, I looked forward to weekend visits with you. The only thing that mattered was that we were together. At the time, I didn't understand that you were giving me the gift of quality time with you. We spent endless hours at the park and you never got tired of pushing me in the swing, no matter how many times I asked.

You never raised your voice at me and you always showed your love without hesitation. You often said, "You can't show a child too much love".

I salute you and I thank God because of all the fathers in the world, He made you just for me, and, as the oldest of your four children, I confidently speak for all of us when I say, "you've been a great father".

I love you,

Bonnye

Introduction

I was approximately 10 years old when my parents separated. I remember the day we moved out like it was yesterday. They eventually divorced. When my parents separated, my mother moved my brother and me to an unfamiliar neighborhood and enrolled us in a new school, where I tried my best to fit and find acceptance among the other girls, but it wasn't easy. My mother did her best to ensure that my brother and I adjusted well to what was to be our new normal: living without my father in the home. I remember writing letters to my father to let him know how much I missed him. I never mailed them, but, somehow, I felt better once I put my feelings on paper.

I was constantly ridiculed at the new school because my body was more developed than many of the other girls, so I was the object of endless teasing. Shortly after arriving at the new school, a group of girls cornered me in the girl's bathroom and pinned me against the wall, raised up my blouse and then laughed uncontrollably, when they saw that I was wearing a bra. They ran out of the bathroom and left me standing there by myself. I was humiliated and ashamed. That was the first of many tearful days at the new school.

By the time I entered high school, I was more confident and because I was outgoing, I had plenty of friends. One thing I noticed was that many of my classmates and friends were also being raised without their father in the home. I didn't realize then what a profound effect a father's absence had on children until I began working with teens years later.

Although my parents divorced when I was a child, it wasn't as common then for parents to get divorced. Children of divorce are impacted. Studies have shown that girls raised without their father in the home are more likely to experiment with premarital sex at an early age. Many of those sexual encounters result in unplanned pregnancy, which is what happened to me. I found myself pregnant and scared at the age of 16. It wasn't until I was older that I realized that in my attempt to be accepted, I had engaged in sexual intimacy before I was mentally ready to do so.

Knowing how significant a father's love and involvement is to the development and well-being of children, the idea for this book of love letters from fathers to daughters was born.

What began as a compilation of letters for this book, evolved into a beautiful labor of love. The men who participated in writing these letters are from different walks of life: pastors, educators, church deacons, a pilot, a musician, a military officer, military veterans, entrepreneurs, a retired law enforcement officer, an air traffic controller and many others. The common factor that unites them is that they are all fathers with daughters or they were raised with sisters whom they love dearly.

It is my hope that each of these letters will fulfill the intent for which they were written, which is to encourage young ladies to understand their value and worth and not to settle for anything less than who God has created them to be.

These letters reveal the heart and love of the men who wrote them. May you feel the love and acceptance of God through these letters.

Model the behavior you would like
to see in others

Table of Contents

Know Your Worth   K. Mulkey…   1

You Make Me Proud   V. Green…   6

God's Creation   J. Calas…   10

Someone Cares   T. Dixon…   13

You Changed Me   C. Judie…   16

You Have My Heart   C. McShan…   19

You are Strong   A. Garcia…   22

Sweet Daughter   L. Douglas…   26

You're a Queen   C. Rogers…   30

You're Special   R. Shephard…   32

You Deserve the Best   N. Kimbrough..   35

The Perfect Gift   V. Williams…   39

Thank God for You   T. Johnson…   42

I Love You   R. Rosado…   45

Daddy's Girl   O. L. Douglas.. 49

Inner Beauty   M. Darling…   52

Live and Grow   M. Massey…   55

Eight Things   E. Davis…   59

Endless Love   M. McKinney..   63

No Limits   L. Stenson…   66

Bright Future   J. Wallace…   72

Dream Big   V. Matthews...   75

I Knew   D. Emerson...   79

Reach for the Stars   A. Burkett...   81

Live Your Purpose   C. Mackey...   84

You Matter   V. Hedgeman...   87

Look Up   C. Marshall...   90

One of a Kind   E. Robinson...   93

Success is Yours   G. Young...   97

Daddy's Little Girl   H. Simon...   100

You Make me Proud   V. Mayon   102

Thank You   M. Potts   105

You matter!

Know Your Worth

Dear Daughter,

You may have gone through a portion of your life wondering, wishing and having questions related to your father. Where is he? Why did he leave me? Does he love me? Will he ever come back? These questions are normal and you should never feel guilty about thinking or asking them. It's my sincere prayer that these questions will not make you doubt yourself as a young lady. Neither you nor I can know what was going on in your father's head and why certain decisions were made (only God truly knows) and you may never know.

I've been blessed to be a father of three daughters, but for a few moments, allow me to speak to you as "a father". Every father knows that he has limitations and cannot be everything that you would need in your life. This is not because he doesn't care, but he understands you need MORE. So, you need to take the remainder of these words to heart.

You are fearfully and wonderfully made in God's image and likeness. You are a beautiful and wonderful creation of God, the Heavenly Father.

If you've ever been in awe of the beauty of creation, just know that when God created you, He was in 'awe' of YOU!

1

There is not another person quite like you, so embrace your uniqueness.

Endeavor to be the 'best you can be', instead of comparing yourself with what media and others deem as beautiful or acceptable. You are wonderful as you are, so love yourself.

My last statement is possible because God loves you. There is something called "unconditional love" - love with no conditions. This means that you're loved not because you have been good, nor, does it mean that if you do something wrong, you are no longer loved. God loves you this way because He *is* Love. As a young lady, your heart longs to be loved, but that doesn't begin with a "boyfriend' and it will not end with a husband. The love of a man will bless you as He learns to love you as Christ loves the church, but only God's love can satisfy and fulfill you - remember this.

Be a young lady of virtue and character. Many will allow themselves to live according to what others say, or feel is right, opposed to what God's Word says is the truth and that is what's right. Your character is developed when you consistently make right choices whether you're alone or with others. It will make you strong and cause you to stand out from the crowd.

Above all else, please know that you are the apple of God's eye - YOU ARE SPECIAL AND YOU ARE LOVED!

~~

Pastor Ken Mulkey and his wife, Angel, have lovingly raised three daughters and their much-loved brother.

Reflections from Sharon's Heart

Embrace and appreciate who you are. You are unique and there's no one else like you.

"For am I now seeking the approval of man, or of God? Or am I trying to please man? If I were still trying to please man, I would not be a servant of Christ" (Galatians 1:10, English Standard Version)

List Three Things You Like About Yourself

1._____

2. _____

3. _____

You Make Me Proud

Dear Princess,

This letter is to let you know how proud I am of the awesome young lady that you have become. You are truly a gift from GOD. The LORD's grace shined bright upon us when HE blessed us with someone as lovable as you. Your warm, caring spirit is second to none. You're beautiful, intelligent and compassionate and your distinct character touches my heart. It always brings tears of joy when you use your God-given gifts and talents for HIS glory. I can only imagine the great blessings that are in store for you.

You've listened and reaped the benefits of prayerful instructions. Thank you for not growing up too fast and for making wise choices in selecting your friends. Life brings about challenges that we don't always understand and sometimes we make mistakes, some of which cause us to look down on ourselves. I want you to hold your head up, knowing that you're highly esteemed and you're a conqueror, victorious and capable of achieving whatever you want to achieve. Satan's job is to confuse and disappoint, but seek GOD's guidance and HE will direct you to a place of joy, peace and happiness. The devil will also attempt to make you angry but always give a soft answer, it will keep drama at bay.

Remember, victory comes through trusting GOD. He will never let you down nor will He forsake you, so no matter what life throws at you, always stay focused on what is positive. Love yourself, believe in yourself and stay true to God and yourself and know that I'm here to listen to all of your concerns, to pick you up when you're down, to love and encourage you and to celebrate all of your accomplishments.

Blessings to you, my beloved. Continue to make me proud as you grow into the beautiful woman God has ordained you to be.

Love Always.

~~

Pastor Victor Green and his wife, Debra, have one adult daughter.

Reflections from Sharon's Heart

It's ok if you don't fit in with the crowd. Be bold enough to stand out from the crowd.

"Do not conform to the pattern of this world, but be transformed by the renewing of your mind" (Romans 12:2, New International Version).

What do you do when you're lonely?

1._____

2. _____

3. _____

God's Creation

Dear Princess,

You are to be honored for you are a Princess; loved and adored.

I hope your days have been filled with fun and memorable experiences. When the weather is warm, it allows time to explore nature that is all around us. This summer I enjoyed bird watching a variety of birds of all shapes and colors. One of the lessons learned from bird watching is that you do not have to travel far to experience the beauty and wonder of God's creation.

The simplest things in life can be the most precious things in life and I encourage you to take a moment and observe the world around you. The flowers, the trees, the clouds and even the insects are fun to observe and provide hours of fun and excitement. I encourage you to take some time with nature and enjoy all it has to give.

In Christ's Love.

~~

Jim Calas and his wife, Susan, have five adult children and 11 grandchildren.

Reflections from Sharon's Heart

Replace negative thoughts and negative talk with positivity and love.

"Death and life are in the power of the tongue, and those who love it will eat its fruits" (Proverbs 18:21, English Standard Version)

What are you strengths?

1._____

2. _____

3. _____

Someone Cares

Dear Precious One,

I hope that things a going well for you and if they are not, please let someone know. It is important that you have every opportunity to reach the goals and dreams you have for your life and getting help from someone that you know cares for you, will make the journey to success much easier.

You are growing into a beautiful young woman; brilliant, beautiful and full of energy and ready to take on the world. I am so proud you and of how you are living your life. Being a leader and setting good examples shows there is a great future ahead of you. It is amazing that at your age you understand how valuable you are and the importance of your success.

Continue to believe in yourself, trust God, and work hard for what you want. You deserve the best this world has to offer and no one can stop you from getting it as long as you don't quit. You are learning how to choose friends that have the same focus on succeeding in school and in life, and that is very important. Surrounding yourself with the right friends, teachers, and adults will help to stay on the shortest path to your dreams.

Let's switch gears and discuss boys. They are always in a hurry; they never really know what they want at first and it takes them a long time to get themselves together. So what does that mean to you? Take it slow with the boys. Keep them at a friend level and over time you will see what is really in their heart. Respect is the key to allowing any boy to be around you. Remember, God made a lot of boys and you can have your choice, so pick the best and settle for nothing less.

I am so proud to know you are doing something positive for your future. You are a smart and very talented young lady with a lot to offer the world. I am happy you understand how important you are and know that your dreams can come true as long as you are willing to do the work. Remember that God has placed in you the ability to achieve whatever you can conceive as being the best life for yourself. Trust who you are, believe in yourself, never be afraid to make a mistake and work hard for what you want and you will succeed.

I am so proud of you and love you with all my heart. My prayer is that you are protected each day, have success in everything you do and that hyour life is filled with joy daily.

I love you so much!

~~

Tony Dixon and his wife, Tracy, have two adult children and two grandchildren.

Reflections from Sharon's Heart

Love yourself a little more each day.

"For no one has ever hated his own body, but he nourishes and tenderly cares for it, as the Messiah does the church" (Ephesians 5:29, International Standard Version).

You Changed Me

Dear Precious Daughter,

I remember when I first found out that I was going to be a father. I was nervous, but excited. I was nervous because I had no idea what to expect. I was excited because I knew that your birth would change my life...for the better.

The moment you were born, I wanted to protect you from everything and from ca. I jokingly told myself that I wouldn't allow you to date until you were 30, because I didn't want you to grow up and not need me. I eventually realized that you'll always need me: You need me to support your dreams. You need me to inspire you to be your best. You need me to love you unconditionally. You need me to always be there for you. And I realize that I also need you.

I am proud of the young lady that you have become and I encourage you to give yourself permission to spread your wings and soar as high as you can. Don't place any limitations on yourself, because I never will. I believe in you and I know that there is greatness inside of you waiting to be awakened. Dream big. Walk confidently. Believe in yourself. Life is a beautiful gift, so handle it prayerfully. I love you.

~~

Carl Judie and his wife, Sharon, have five adult children and four grandchildren.

Reflections from Sharon's Heart

Find what makes you happy and do it.

"Take delight in the Lord, and He will give you the desires of your heart" (Psalm 37:4, New International Version

What are your goals for the next three years?

1._____

2._____

3._____

4._____

5._____

You Have My Heart

Dear Princess,

When you were born, it was one the most blessed days of my life. A new chapter was beginning for your mom and me, and we were so excited. I had been waiting outside the delivery room and the nurses came and said there were complications with your delivery. The doctors were concerned because Mommy wasn't dilating properly and they would have to deliver you by Caesarian section. Tears were rolling down my face, until I could barely see. I wanted you and mommy to be alright. The nurses were very reassuring and told me things would be OK.

I prayed, of course, and shortly afterwards the nurses brought me the most beautiful baby I had ever seen, my little "bird'. I have loved you from that day and my love grows for you every day. My pride in you is growing also, as you've become a beautiful woman, with compassionate spiritual gifts that bless all that come in contact with you.

You are an expression of the love I have for Mommy, and I thank God for you. A father couldn't be prouder of his daughter than I am of you. In your spiritual walk, I see the light of Jesus Christ and He uses you to minister to so many of your family and friends. You pray for us, you counsel us, you take care of us. The future is bright for you and as a godly woman, you are an example for others.

This is my love letter to you, "Bird", and as you know, you have my heart, Daddy's Girl. And next to Mommy, you are the love of my Life.

With love always.

~~

Pastor Chris McShan and his wife, Joyce, have five adult children and five grandchildren.

Reflections from Sharon's Heart

Don't be quick to judge others. Instead, get to know them and understand them.

"Do not judge others, and you will not be judged. Do not condemn others, or it will all come back against you. Forgive others, and you will be forgiven" (Luke 6:37, New Living Translation)

You Are Strong!

Dear Princess Warrior,

It's amazing how a young woman can be both a princess (knowing that she deserves the best) and a warrior (willing to fight for what she knows she deserves) at the same time. I write to you to introduce this concept to you and to help you understand how to kick life's butt.

Have you ever thought that you deserve more? Have you ever thought that there's more to life then where you are now? The truth is this...there is a lot more to life than what you think there is, but I want to share a truth with you. The greatest things in life don't always come easy. You need to fight for them. If you want these great things, you need to be a Warrior, but not the type of Warrior that fights people, but fights the things in life that are super strong... things like failure, disappointment, anger, hurt and pain. Those are obstacles that will try to hold you back. Be assured that you can overcome your past, your memories of your past and insecurities because of your past and any hopelessness you may feel. Believe in yourself! I believe in you. I believe that the Princess in you is why you smile, dream big and have hope.

I believe the warrior in you is the reason why your dreams will come true. Dream like a Princess and fight like a Warrior.

~~

Pastor Art Garcia and his wife, Christina, have two daughters.

What makes you happy?

1._____

2. _____

3. _____

4. _____

5. _____

Reflections from Sharon's Heart

Always look for the best in others.

"Love each other with genuine affection, and take delight in honoring each other" (Romans 12:10, New Living Translation)

Daughter, Sweet Daughter!

Do remember to put and keep God first in everything that you do.

Don't compromise your walk to gain the company of others.

Do remember that you are valuable and were bought with a price.

Don't cheapen yourself to gain affection.

Do good for everyone that you encounter.

Don't let your kindness be mistaken for weakness.

Do strive for excellence in every area of your life.

Don't expect perfection from yourself or from others.

Do expect the best that life has to offer.

Don't settle for less than what God has for your life.

Do continue to move forward when you experience failures in your life.

Don't wallow in self-pity when you fall short of the mark.

Do live as though tomorrow is not promised.

Don't fail to plan as though tomorrow will never come.

Do laugh so hard that tears fall from your eyes.

Don't forget that bitter tears can sometimes wash away pain.

Do travel and experience the world.

Don't forget from where you've come.

Do the best that you can, for as long as you can, for as many as you can.

Don't forget that you can't please everyone.

~~

O. Lee Douglas, Jr., and his wife, Greta, have three adult sons.

Reflections from Sharon's Heart

Many choices that you make today will affect you for the rest of your life. Choose wisely.

"Let us choose for us that which is right. Let us know among ourselves what is good" (Job 34:4, World English Bible)

What's the best advice you've received?

1._____

2. _____

3. _____

You Are a Queen

Dear Queen,

What can I say to you? Only the words of life your ears deserve: From my heart, I want you to know that I love you and I have been praying for you every day of your life.

I want you know that you are beautiful in every way. You are beautiful because God created you, He saw all that he had made, and it was very good. You were made in the glorious image of God. He made you with a conscience. He made you with a soul. He made you in original righteousness. God made you to be His. He wants to be the superior lover of your soul.

People may fail you, friends may abandon you, but God will never leave you nor forsake you. He died for you. He shed His blood to pay the penalties for your sins and desires that you repent and believe in Him. Nothing in this life is greater than a relationship with God, the Almighty LORD that holds the essence of your very life in His hand. Look for a husband that loves and believes in Jesus, and is not ashamed of God and one who will love you unconditionally. Look for a man that will honor your body and not guide you into premarital sex. Look for a man that will commit in holy matrimony to you until you die.

Look for a husband that will sacrifice everything to lovingly serve you; a man that will provide for you, care for your thoughts and listen to your heart. And with this man of God, you will build a legacy, a generation that will know God and your children will raise up and call you blessed.

I love you and can't think of anything greater to tell you than these words.

~~

Rev. Cory Rogers and his wife, Marleena, have four children.

You Are Special

Dear Precious Daughter,

I am writing to let you know that you are special, so please don't ever forget that. God didn't make you like anyone else and don't let anyone tell you that you are anything less than what you believe to be true about yourself.

You are a beautiful young lady created by God. You were created for excellence in every area of your life, so long as you trust Him and believe in the gifts and the talents that He has placed in you. My dear, notice that I said "the gifts and talents that He has placed in you". That means that His blessings are already at work in your life. They are just waiting for you to unlock them. Your faith in God is the key that unlocks His favor. Always remember that you are fearfully and wonderfully made. God took great time and care to create you and only you. There is no one else like you among His creation. You are special, so embrace the fact that you are beautiful, different, loving, caring, and yes, sometimes you can be *mouthy*. It's just you. I love you, but please remember that above all, God loves you because it's YOU! Never give up on your dreams and ambitions!

~~

Rev. Russell Shephard and his wife, MaCasha, have two children.

Reflections from Sharon's Heart

No matter where you find yourself in life, you are never alone.

"Fear not, for I am with you; be not dismayed, for I am your God; I will strengthen you, I will help you, I will uphold you with my righteous right hand." (Isaiah 41:10, English Standard Version)

What habit or habits do you want to break?

1._____

2. _____

3. _____

You Deserve the Best

Dear Daughter,

Where do I begin? From the day you took your first breath, I loved you.

I wish I could take credit, but where you are now is not all because of me. God ordained for you to be in my life and where you are. It's funny now to think of it, but when you were born, I was really afraid. There's no manual for fatherhood, but we made it this far.

When I look at you, there is a joy that can't be explained, for you are the epitome of what any father prays that his daughter will grow to be. You're smart, you're considerate and you're a good example for other young women. Your list of qualities are long and well-deserved. I know everything hasn't always been easy for you, but you've endured. That speaks volumes about your character. Remember, it's not what you do in the eyes of the public, but it's what you stand for when the lights are not shining on you. Keep your integrity, my sweet child, because it hasn't failed you yet. Keep God first and any dream that you have is possible according to God's word.

I know I often go and on about how I feel about you, but words can't adequately express what a gift you are to our family. Your smile affects my heart and soul to the point that I can't help but to stand and stick out my chest because of how proud I am to call you my daughter.

It's been said that a man's daughter is the apple of his eye, but you are an entire orchard that runs over with sweetness that surpasses my wildest imagination. Who knew that you would become such a phenomenal person? Time will prove how great you really are!

My prayer is that you'll never turn from God, for one day I won't be around to watch over you. That's alright because until that time, I will keep loving you with all that I am.

With all my love.

~~

Rev. Nathan Kimbrough, Sr., and his wife, Linda, have three adult children and one granddaughter.

Reflections from Sharon's Heart

Always tell the truth and you won't have to remember what you said.

"When you tell the truth, justice is done, but lies lead to injustice" (Proverbs 12:17, New International Version).

What is your favorite quote? Why?

_____

_____

_____

_____

_____

You Are the Perfect Gift

Dear Daughter,

The first thing I want to say is, "I love you and God loves you". When God brought you into my life, you were one of His greatest blessings. I couldn't have asked for a better gift from heaven.

Many questions flooded my mind, including, "Will I be a good parent?" "Will I teach her right from wrong?" "Will I instill good values in her life?" "Will she remember what I taught her when I'm not in her presence?" "Will she know when to say no and not be a follower, but a leader?"

There are so many things in life that I need to prepare you for and the first thing that comes to mind is character. What is character? It's the way a person thinks and feels and behaves, which helps to build your character. There are so many questions that you will have that only a man can answer. So I hope you will call on me to help you when that time arrives. If I'm not available, there is another source that is always available: God.

In the Bible, there are scriptures that deal with any situation you can think of or need. People refer to the Bible as "The Good Book". Many times I've referred to scriptures for advice.

Remember these words and plant them in your heart: I LOVE YOU and God loves you.

~~

Vernon Williams and his wife, Bobbi, have 5 adult children and 13 grandchildren and four great-grandchildren.

Reflections from Sharon's Heart

Be comfortable with who you are and don't be afraid to be yourself.

"Do not let your adorning be external—the braiding of hair and the putting on of gold jewelry, or the clothing you wear— but let your adorning be the hidden person of the heart with the imperishable beauty of a gentle and quiet spirit, which in God's sight is very precious" (1 Peter 3:3-4, English Standard Version)

.

I Thank God for You

Dear Daughter,

I was sitting and thinking and remembering how I was waiting for you. Wondering what you would be like. What you would look like and who you would become.

I remember the very first time I saw you and how it made me feel. I have experienced so many different feelings and emotions in life, so many highs and lows. In everything that has happened to me in my lifetime, I never had a feeling like what I felt the first time I saw you. At first I thought, *she is so beautiful*. But that feeling gave way to the deepest feeling of love that I have ever had. You were one of the most wonderful beings that I had ever seen and I wondered how I could be so blessed to have you? Then, that feeling gave way to a feeling of fear. I thought, "She is so sweet and so innocent. I need to protect her from anything that could ever change her." I wanted you to stay young forever.

Inside all of those emotions I was experiencing back then, I never thought you could mean more to me in my life. I was never so wrong. I never thought that you would grow up to be so incredibly beautiful. You have grown to become the most amazing woman. Every time I see you I'm overwhelmed with how much you have grown into a perfect woman.

42

Now it is me reaching out to you for support and advice. The Bible says, "God so loved the world that He gave His begotten Son". Well, after having you for a daughter, I can say that God so loved "ME" that He sent me the most beautiful and loving daughter. You make me so happy, sweetheart.

I love you with all of my heart. Thank you for letting me be your Dad.

~~

Terence Johnson has seven children and three grandchildren.

Reflections from Sharon's Heart

Everybody is not like you, so try to understand where they're coming from and love them where they are.

"Be tolerant with one another and forgive one another whenever any of you has a complaint against someone else. You must forgive one another just as the Lord has forgiven you" (Colossians 3:13, Good News Translation)

I Love You

Dear Daughter,

I'm writing this letter to you because you've been on my mind lately. Tomorrow is not promised and there comes a time when you have to let the ones you love know what's in your heart.

I often find myself thinking about you as the little girl I held in my arms vowing to protect you from any harm or danger; to insulate you from the negative associations that lurks around everything we do. All the while knowing I would have to let you go soon and accept the role of observer, and hopefully, advisor. I often worried that my firm, but fair discipline would affect our relationship as you grew into a young woman. I thank God that love held us together.

I know at times you may have felt I let you down and vice versa. But in spite of those bumps in the road, I thank God we've remained present in each other's lives. We may not have always agreed with one another, but we respected each other's viewpoint. I know this because you chose to put God at the head of your life and there would be little for me to worry about. Situations and challenges always worked themselves out for the good.

You have made me a very proud father as I watched you grow through every challenge that you faced and overcame (with a little help from Dad).

Please know that whatever happens in this life, I am always Daddy and I will always be here for you. I love you as much now as I did when your little hand squeezed mine for the first time. We have a bond that no man can sever for as long as I live and breathe.

I love you.

~~

Ruben Rosado and his wife, Tina, have two children and one granddaughter.

Reflections from Sharon's Heart

Do not trade your dignity for popularity.

"The eyes of the Lord are upon the righteous, and His ears are open unto their cry" (Colossians 3:13, Good News Translation)

What habit or habits do you want to break?

1._____

2._____

3._____

Daddy's Girl

One of the happiest days of my life was when I laid eyes on you for the very first time. I was in the Air Force and stationed in Japan, so I didn't actually meet you face-to-face for the first time until you were 9 months old. Fortunately for me, your mother always showed you pictures of me, so you had an idea of what I looked like. The first time we met, you reached for me and smiled and I knew that you were (and still are) a daddy's girl.

What I immediately noticed was that your personality was an even mix of mine and your mother's. You were inquisitive and intelligent. Sincere and strong. Talkative and thoughtful. Sassy and sentimental. Funny and fascinating. You were perfect!

When I think back to when you were a little girl, I remember how it warmed my heart to see how you cared about those who were less fortunate. You wanted to give them money or food and wanted to make sure they were ok and that they had a warm place to stay. You also loved animals. There were times when our backyard looked like a pet motel because of the lost and injured animals that you brought home and tried to nurse back to health.

Birds and dogs were your favorites. You loved animals so much that at one time, your dream was to become a veterinarian. You probably thought that I forgot that was your heart's desire. I didn't forget.

You have always had a big heart and you've always loved everybody. You quickly became friends with total strangers and from what I hear, you are still that way, even now. You were always friendly and wanted to be friends with everyone you met. Many of the traits that you now possess were evident when you were young.

Watching you grow into the woman you are today was an interesting journey for both of us. Every father wishes his daughter would remain a little girl forever and it was no different for me. When you were a teenager and began receiving attention from teenaged boys, I cringed because I knew there would come a day when I would no longer be your number one guy. There were many times when I wanted to turn back the hands of time and carry you on my shoulders again, but time doesn't stand still, so I think of those times and cherish those moments.

I want you to know how proud I am to be your father. Although you are grown, with a family of your own and you are several thousand miles away, I want you to know that I love you and you will always be daddy's girl.

I love you.

~~

O. L. Douglas, Sr., is Sharon Y. Judie's father. He and his wife, Yvonne, have four adult children, seven grandchildren, and two great-grandchildren.

Reflections from Sharon's Heart

T.H.I.N.K. before you speak. Ask yourself if it's:

True

Helpful

Inspiring

Necessary

Kind

"Do not let any unwholesome talk come out of your mouths, but only what is helpful for building others up according to their needs, that it may benefit those who listen." (Ephesians 4:29, New International Version)

Your Inner Beauty

Dear Daughter,

I'm glad I have this chance to talk to you. I am fortunate to have you in my life. Sometimes we do not agree with each other, but that's not what life is about. Life is about how we feel about each other. Life is about respect for each other. Life is feeling good about us.

I am so proud of you for the things you have accomplished. I think you have a lot to offer this world and you will make a great impact on our lives.

When you look at yourself in the mirror, I hope you see your inner beauty. God has made you like no one else. He has made you a caring and passionate person. Let no one tell you, "You are not beautiful" because you are beautiful.

Set your goals high and try to attain them. I look forward to watching you grow in the Lord and in life.

Thank you for the opportunity to know you and be part of your life.

Stay loving, stay caring and stay beautiful.

~~

Michael Darling and his wife, Sheila, have one daughter.

What changes do you want in your life?

1._____

2. _____

3. _____

Reflections from Sharon's Heart

You are beautiful just as you are.

"You are altogether beautiful, my love; there is no flaw in you" (Song of Solomon 4:7, English Standard Version)

Live and Grow

Dearest Daughter,

I hope this letter finds you well and prospering in the ever abiding love of God. It seems strange and somewhat frightening to write to you about matters that are of deep concern to me. Letters are for the courageous explorers of the mind and soul. For those willing to honestly examine and reveal with heartfelt clarity the matters that encourage and trouble the heart. I have not always permitted this level of vulnerability and I must admit it is much easier to attempt to walk before you in integrity than to reveal that I often have no idea of the certainty of my next steps. I simply trust, as you must, in God. Trusting God has revealed a simple truth to me that I am compelled to share with you: We must live and we must grow.

My sweet, sweet child - you must live. Moment by moment you are becoming a product of your experiences. Your hopes, dreams and frustrations will all serve to reinforce or combat the rich deposit that God has placed in you. When we live, we embrace the day. We trust God for provision and we move unapologetically from circumstance to circumstance, fully aware that each will be a unique building block of our character.

We declare victory over everything that would make us stand still, mortified by fear. You must live as though you have fully accepted both your power and potential. You must live as if you are set upon meeting the multiple and varied appointments that destiny has scheduled with you. Live and you will know that you are alive.

Grow. Do not forget that life and growth come hand-in-hand. Growth is the rudder that propels life. It is the evidence that life, in all of its splendor and complexity, is present. Pursue it in earnest and it will lead you to an extraordinary and uncommon peace. Do not refuse an opportunity to expand and excite your mind as it will ignite your growth. Do not be intimidated or directed by others who try to dictate where, when, and how much you can grow.

Lastly, be the tender flower beat upon by the rain that has the courage to endure and the wisdom to know that each drop comes as an answered prayer to nourish her roots, replenish her thirst and prepare her for the coming sun. My sweet girl, live and grow!

~~

Mark Massey has three daughters.

What are you most proud of accomplishing?

1._____

2. _____

3. _____

Reflections from Sharon's Heart

Don't be a follower. Be a good leader.

"Don't let anyone think less of you because you are young. Be an example to all believers in what you say, in the way you live, in your love, your faith, and your purity" (1 Timothy 4:12, New Living Translation)

Eight Things

Dear Princess,

I would like to share eight things that you can do to successfully prepare for your future:

1) Work hard academically and take time to determine your favorite subject areas.

2) Explore different aspects in the Arts that interest you, such as learning to read sheet music and/or learning to play an instrument.

   a. Learn a particular style of dance (modern dance, ballet, hip hop, etc.). Other expressions of art can also include learning to paint or sculpting, etc., so be open to learning something new. Develop your skills in your favorite art form. You may be surprised that you're really good at one or more.

3) Participate in a variety of different sports to discover your favorite sport. Once you figure out which you like best, practice hard and long to perfect your skills so that you can excel.

4) Interview your parents and grandparents and ask them about their major accomplishments and about how major events in their lives have impacted them. You can take what you learn from them and write of your family history. Ask how and where your parents and grandparents met and create your family tree. Research the race and culture of your ancestors and their major accomplishments. There are a lot of interesting facts waiting to be discovered.

5) Read the biography of someone famous that you admire.

6) Memorize your favorite poem.

7) Research colleges that you are interested in attending for Arts or Science Degrees (Associates, Bachelors, Master's, and PhD), as well as the majors and subjects those colleges offer that you are interested in pursuing, and identify professions that may be of interest to you after you graduate.

8) Write a timeline of your future education and career path that you are considering to follow and be specific.

Example:

2020-I will be a freshman at UC Berkeley
2021- I will be a sophomore
2022- I will be a junior
2023- I will be a senior
2024-I will graduate with BS from UC Berkeley
in journalism and work for NBC as a reporter
2026- I will get married
2027- We will save money to buy a house
2029- We will have our first child

~~

Earnie Davis has one daughter.

Reflections from Sharon's Heart

Don't rush into dating. Focus on yourself, because there's plenty of time to date as you get more mature.

Never allow anyone rush you into doing anything you don't want to do.

"Submit yourselves therefore to God. Resist the devil, and he will flee from you" (James 4:7, English Standard Version.

Endless Love

To My Dear Daughter,

I hope this letter finds you in good health. I'm writing this to let you know how much I love you, and the smart, beautiful young lady you have become.

I'm so proud of your academic accomplishments and the way you've shown responsibility and maturity. I've watched you grow from my little baby girl-running around and getting into things. I remember teaching you how to ride a bike and how to swim. I remember how proud I was as you started to receive your awards in school and you continued throughout high school. Watching you graduate and hearing your name called was truly a magical moment; in that instance I flashed back to all those earlier memories. You will be going off to school soon and I just hope some of the things that your mother and I have shown you will help you in life.

Try to remember that it's hard to be a leader and easy to be a follower, but the results for the leader are his or her own because they made that choice.

The results for the follower are dropped on them because they chose to stay with the group letting someone else dictate what they do. Always keep your eyes open to the world around you. Sometimes the right thing to do may be hard, but just know that I believe in your decision-making and I back you 100 %.

I know I've told you before that I might not agree with all of your decisions, some will be good and some not, but I will never stop loving you.

~~

Mack McKinney and his wife, LaCresia, have one daughter.

Reflections from Sharon's Heart

Take time and enjoy your childhood. You will be an adult soon enough. Slow down and learn all you can so that you can make wise decisions.

"Young people, it's wonderful to be young! Enjoy every minute of it. Do everything you want to do; take it all in. But remember that you must give an account to God for everything you do" (Ecclesiastes 11:9, New Living Translation)

No Limits

Dear Princess & Future Queen,

I write this letter to let you know that you are truly a precious gift from God. Each day as you grow older, wiser, more beautiful and start to blossom into a woman - I cannot help but smile. I realize life is not easy and certainly full of ups and downs but remember the joys of life absolutely outweigh life's trials and tribulations.

You are capable of doing whatever you want to do in life; never let anyone tell you that you are not smart enough, pretty enough, or strong enough to achieve your dreams. Pursue your passion and the money will follow. Always be a leader and innovator; set the example. Stand tall and proud! Show kindness and love to those who deserve it and be the one who will hold those who are misguided, confused, and on the wrong path accountable for their actions. Sometimes, being a friend means telling folks, who are clearly messing up their lives, that they have to get themselves together and stay focused on doing what is right. Trust God, pray and ask for guidance as you approach each new endeavor in life.

Study hard, in and out of school, so that your mind is an oracle of knowledge that you can use and share with others who may need inspiration, guidance and wisdom.

Work with your hands (sewing, knitting, origami) and never be too much of a modern woman to know how to prepare good meals, grow vegetables and fruits, read classic and sci-fi books for fun, and keep your mind flexible by solving puzzles, (Sudoku, Magic Squares, Tangrams, crossword puzzles, mathematical riddles).

Take care of your body through prayer, meditation, healthy eating and regular exercise. It's been said, "in life there are only a few decisions that are life changing and set the course for the rest of your life". One of those, and probably the most important, is selecting the right mate when you are ready. It is my prayer for you that I have set the example of a man that you would consider marrying in the way I have treated your mother in showing her my unwavering love, devotion, faithfulness, and complete support as she works towards her dreams and has supported me in mine.

If a man does not want you to achieve your dreams, does not want you to follow the word of God, does not love you unconditionally, does not understand the importance of being loving and kind, is OK with living with you without marrying you and has no vision for where he would like to go or how he would lead his potential future wife and family, he is not the man for you.

If you don't remember anything else, please remember these simple words... "The most critical decision you will make in life is who you decide to marry." Along those lines, be a Godly woman of impeccable character that sets the bar so high that only the most noble of young men would even consider approaching you. Players, thugs, liars, knuckle draggers, wanna-be's and other clowns are never boyfriend or marriage material no matter how much they have or claim to have. You want a do-right, educated, God-fearing man that even scares the Devil straight! Once you find that do-right man, be a loving wife who is free, unselfish, and giving to your husband.

As you get older, the other critical decisions you will have to make involve things such as what career path you choose after college, who do you accept into your inner circle of friends, how do you and your husband want to raise the kids (your parenting philosophy), how much money you should save (start young and it will pay off years down the road).

As you start your career as a professional, your thoughts will focus more on whether you should attend graduate school (post Bachelor's degrees), how to handle life's changes and difficulties (I pray your faith is firmly rooted in Jesus Christ and know that God will guide you through life's ups and downs), is there a good time to change careers (if you choose to do so) and what kind of involvement do you want to have in your community (volunteering).

I pray these words of wisdom find favor in your heart and provide general guidance as you maneuver through the landmines of life. Set your life course, sail it, rest when you must, but never quit, never surrender and stay true to our God, your family, friends and those you hold dearest. As a martial artist, I try to live my life by the tenants of my base art Tae Kwon Do. The tenets of *Courtesy, Self-Control, Integrity, Perseverance, and Indomitable Spirit* are not bad principles by which to live. Please know I am very proud of you and know you will make the right decisions and most importantly, don't be afraid to fail. Failure is truly one of the best teaching tools in life.

I hope you know how much you are loved.

~~

Lee Stenson and his wife, Stephanie, have one daughter.

Do you follow your heart or your head? Why?

_____

_____

_____

_____

Reflections from Sharon's Heart

Others may try to distract you to keep you from reaching your full potential. Stay focused and you will succeed.

"I can do all things through Him who strengthens me"
(Philippians 4:11, English Standard Version.

Your Bright Future

There comes a time in life when we all can use a word of encouragement. To everything there is a season and a time to every purpose under heaven. Listen to your heart and love yourself continually. I have watched you grow up and become the beautiful young lady that you are today. You are ready to contribute to society, making our world a better place to live.

Love yourself and love life with all your heart, your mind, and your soul. Never forget who you are as you go through life's journeys. Be at peace with yourself and where you are every moment of your life. Keep your heart pure and enjoy your own company. Know that you are loved and are very capable to accomplish great things. Focus your attention on all that is good. Strive to achieve that which is better. Embrace every challenge knowing that from within lies the strength that will enable you to overcome any obstacle. Don't be afraid to take chances or make mistakes from time-to-time. Remember, that to know success is also to know and understand failure.

Always remember that your worth and value are not defined by the standards by which the world establishes, but that your worth and value are based upon those things which are ordained by your Creator.

Learn the secrets of contentment and embrace the surprises that life often brings our way. For not every rock in our pathway is there to trip you up, but may be the steppingstone towards a fulfilling life and achievement of your lifelong dreams and realities.

Make your plans for your future known to those who care about and love you. Know where you are going is only part of the plan of your life. Knowing where you have been and where you are at this very moment is important, too. Should you get a little lost along the way, don't worry because there are people who love and will find you.

All that being said, the final thing I can hope that brings you encouragement is that you are worthy, beautiful, talented and loved. Always be yourself in all things and in all matters. It is in these things that you will find purpose, meaning, fulfillment and joy. And most of all, always remember there is One who loves you daily and continually.

With all my love.

~~

John Wallace and his wife, Donna, have four adult children and 9 grandchildren and one great-grandchild.

Reflections from Sharon's Heart

You may not have everything you want, but be thankful for what you have.

"... for I have learned in whatever situation I am to be content" (Philippians 4:11b, English Standard Version).

Dream Big

Dear Princess,

I hope things are going well. I want to tell you something about you. The only person who defines you is YOU! Don't let anyone else tell you that you are not smart or that there is something that you cannot do or that you are not beautiful.

First, and foremost, you are brilliant. You are as smart and as brilliant as you want to be. There is nothing in the world that if you want to know it, you cannot find the answer. Others may try to tell you that you aren't but you have to know that you are.

Second, know that no one can limit what you can or cannot do. Only you can do that. The only barriers to how high you can climb are the barriers you erect in your mind. If you want something badly enough, you can achieve it. Never give up on your dreams. If you can believe it, you can achieve it.

Finally, know that you are beautiful. Take a moment and look into the mirror. See your eyes, your ears, your nose, and your lips. No one else looks exactly like you or is as beautiful as you. Let no one else define your beauty. Look again and know that you are beautiful.

My Princess, please know that you are brilliant, and there is nothing that you cannot achieve. You are beautiful! You are loved!

~~

Dr. Vincent Matthews and his wife, Yolie, have three adult children and one grandson.

Reflections from Sharon's Heart

Always look for the bright side in every situation.

"This is the day which the LORD hath made; we will rejoice and be glad in it" (Psalm 118:24, King James Version)

What are you passionate about?

_____

_____

_____

_____

I Knew

I knew that I loved you from the first time I laid eyes on you.

I knew that I had to learn how to do your hair. I knew that I had to protect you. I knew that one day I had to let you paint my nails. I knew that I would have to teach you how to ride a bike. I knew that I would have to teach you how to get up when you failed.

I knew that I would have to walk you to school and let go. I knew that one day I would have to walk you down the aisle. I knew that I would have to show you the type of man you should marry. I knew that one day you would grow up. Most important of all -- I knew that I had a daughter to call my own. I couldn't ask for anything more.

~~

Minister Dominic Emerson and his wife, JoAnn, have three children.

Reflections from Sharon's Heart

Live, love, laugh and smile!

"We were filled with laughter, and we sang for joy."
(Psalm 126:2a, New Living Translation)

Reach for the Stars

Hello sweetheart,

I love you and I'm very proud of you.

Watching you grow up has truly been a blessing to me. I love seeing how you always do your best in school as you prepare for life. Remember, life is what you make it and a good education will make a better life for you. Keep pressing forward, dear daughter, even when you face obstacles, do your best to persevere. It's the challenges in life that help build your character and strength. You can do all things through Christ. Keep Him at the center of your life.

Do you know what else is great about you? Yes, you guessed it, it's great when you're kind to others. I admire that quality in you. Sweetheart, I believe we must lend a hand to get a hand. Continue to help others as much as you can. Lean on God to help you know who and how to bless others.

God has a special plan for you and I pray every day that He guides you. Understand that you are uniquely designed for a unique purpose.

I recently saw the movie, "Akeelah and the Bee", which was very entertaining. In the movie, Akeelah's teacher had her read the following: "Our deepest fear is not that we are inadequate. Our deepest fear is that we are powerful beyond measure". We ask ourselves, "Who will I be?" Brilliant, gorgeous, talented and fabulous? Actually, who are you not to be? We were born to make manifest the glory of God that is within us and as we let our own light shine, we unconsciously give other people permission to do the same."

Stay courageous, baby girl, and your dreams will come true.

I love you.

~~

Alvin Burkett and his wife, Raelea, have four adult children and two grandsons.

Reflections from Sharon's Heart

There will be times when you make the wrong decision. Learn from bad decisions and make a better decision next time.

"The godly may trip seven times, but they will get up again. But one disaster is enough to overthrow the wicked" (Proverbs 24:16, New Living Translation)

Live Your Purpose

My dearest daughter,

As I sit here pondering in thought, searching my heart to find the words that I wish to convey to you, my heart aches and longs to know of your beautiful smile that resonates and brings to life all that I've yearned for as a father.

Daughter, I want you to know that I love you and have loved you from the time that you came into this world. Yes, you are Daddy's beloved jewel. In your expression of love, you have taught me to extend the hidden love that I've been afraid to express simply because of my own insecurities.

The radiance of your being enlightens the many who may come across your path. Little do they know that you were shaped into the jewel that you are, long before the foundation of the world.

Your Heavenly Father spoke and you became. Though you may struggle to find your purpose, know that destiny has carved out and manifested itself to ensure that you will be recognized.

Daughter, know that you are special among the special. Never believe that you have nothing to offer. For if that were true, you would have no purpose nor would you have been given the breath of life.

Daughter, strive with purpose and all intent to be the very best that you can, in whatever your calling may be. You are like the still waters that run deep. Your calling will yield and bring to fruition that which is ready to bud within.

Remember, "Adversity does not build character, it reveals it." (Credit: James Lane Allen, Novelist)

I love you. You are Daddy's Girl.

~~

Cal Mackey has six children and 11 grandchildren.

Reflections from Sharon's Heart

Carry yourself like you matter and others will treat you like you matter.

"God never overlooks a single sparrow. And he pays even greater attention to you, down to the last detail – even numbering the hairs on your head!" (Luke 12:6-7, The Message Bible)

You Matter

Dear Precious One,

I had a daughter at the young age of 19, and I've always had full custody of her.

I'll attempt to make a really quick point. As a young lady, you'll likely get attention from boys and it can be confusing because it's attention that you didn't ask for.

But, just know, that as a young lady, it is hard to be seen as a *person* by a guy initially - because a man's eye is so flawed. A man usually won't care about you as a person when he first meets you. We initially care about the physical aspect (such as what you look like) and, maybe we'll end up liking you – later. A single guy usually has multiple girls he's entertaining and if he starts liking one, eventually, there is an unplanned circumstance.

It's a harsh truth but I say this to say: make sure you're *seen.* Seen by your friends and people that you spend time with. If people don't see you as the future business owner, future manager, future evangelist, etc. that you are, then you shouldn't be entertaining them.

Stay great, young queen.

~~

Minister Vada Hedgeman and his wife, Raia, have one daughter.

Reflections from Sharon's Heart

Don't try to be like anyone else. You are unique!

"Yet you, LORD, are our Father. We are the clay, you are the potter; we are all the work of your hand." (Isaiah 64:8, New International Version)

Write an encouraging note to yourself

_____

_____

_____

_____

_____

_____

_____

_____

Look Up

Dear Daughter,

I know you are hurting. At times you feel alone, confused, and like you have no one to turn to. Look up! There is light coming over the horizon. The light that shines throughout all darkness is God. God's light is rising in every moment of your life, and he is saying "daughter come to me, come into the light." It is there and only there where you will be set free. You are trapped in a sea of emotions and God wants to bring you out.

I want you to know that God is your source. When you think of electronics, it has to be connected to some kind of source, whether batteries or a power outlet, in order to work. In the same way, God is our source, so we have to be connected in order to have power and function properly. When you are connected to God, His light begins to shine through you. He is waiting at the door and desperately wants to spend time with you, but it's up to you to open the door. Will you open the door and let Him in your heart? When God enters your heart, He will heal every wound, every hurt, and every disappointment.

Every empty place will be filled. Out of your heart will flow love, joy, and peace. Make this your prayer, say "Father, forgive me for not completely trusting in you; I totally surrender my life to you. Empower me and let me be the light that shines through darkness. Amen!"

You are loved and you are worth more than you can ever imagine.

~~

Curtis Marshall and his wife, Amber, have four children.

Reflections from Sharon's Heart

Time passes quickly, so don't rush to grow up.

Be a good friend to others and choose your friends wisely.

"A friend loves at all times, and a brother is there for times of trouble." (Proverbs 17:17, International Standard Version)

One of a Kind

My dearest daughter,

I want to let you know that I love you and tell you that you are the most beautiful young lady ever created by our Heavenly Father. The Message Bible says in Psalm 139:14-16, "Oh yes, you shaped me first inside, then out; you formed me in my mother's womb. I thank you, High God—you're breathtaking! Body and soul, I am marvelously made! I worship in adoration—what a creation! You know me inside and out, you know every bone in my body; you know exactly how I was made, bit by bit, how I was sculpted from nothing into something. Like an open book, you watched me grow from conception to birth; all the stages of my life were spread out before you, the days of my life all prepared before I'd even lived one day."

These verses tell you that when God made you, He made no mistakes! Moreover, your eyes, ears, lips, hips, feet, hands, brain, and other parts of your body were specially designed just for you. Therefore, when the world, including the media, men, and friends try to place a price tag on your self-worth, tell them that it's impossible, because the Creator, Giver, and Sustainer of life declared you wonderful!

Lastly, I want you to know that there is a perfect plan for your life. However, you must yield your will to His will as He directs you along life's paths. When you hit bumps in the road, please know that both of your daddy's (Heavenly and Earthly) are here to pick you up and to walk alongside you.

Precious daughter, please know that my love for you is never-ending, without judgment, and unconditional.

God Bless you.

~~

Pastor Ed Robinson and his wife, Yvonne, have four adult children.

Reflections from Sharon's Heart

Your parents, teachers and other adults want the best for you. They are not your enemy.

"Let the wise listen and add to their learning, and let the discerning get guidance." (Proverbs 1:5, New International Version)

Describe what a perfect day looks like for you:

_____

_____

_____

_____

_____

Success is Yours

Dear daughter,

You have been socially engineered to fail. Defy the odds and excel.

It hurts my heart to see so many young women led astray by what is portrayed on BET, MTV and Centric by today's divas. Ask the countless number of young ladies whose lives are plagued with STD's, baby momma and daddy drama, *how's it working for you?* Life in the fast-lane is not as glamorous as the media portrays it.

Here are three important lessons designed to defy the trap society has set for you.

1) When fishing, the type of fish you catch is dependent upon the bait you use.

Don't expect to catch a good man who respects you for the beautiful person that you are and the beautiful person that you have the potential to become, if the only bait you use is your body.

By the same token, don't be surprised by the man who takes advantage of the body you put on display. Sex outside of marriage is grossly overrated. That's a fact! Relationships that begin in a bed never get on their feet.

2) Dare to dream. The quality of the life you will live in your 30's and 40's will be dependent on the decisions you make while you are in your teens and 20's. Your life will never become more complicated until you try to share it with someone else. Be sure that you are both mentally and emotionally mature and on your way to financial independence. This process takes time. I know many people who regret not getting an education. But, I don't know anyone that regretted getting one. Make it your goal to pursue a lifetime of learning. At 56, I am still in school.

You must have dreams. You must also WRITE down your goals to accomplish your dreams. What are you passionate about becoming? Dare to dream!!!

3) Life is too short to waste on a fool. As you dare to dream, partner with A MAN that has the same attitude.

We are counting on you to make a difference in your life and the life of your children's children.

You are special and you are loved.

~~

Pastor Greg Young and his wife, Sharay, have eight children and 13 grandchildren.

Reflections from Sharon's Heart

Don't let anyone steal your joy.

"Don't be dejected and sad, for the joy of the LORD is your strength!" (Nehemiah 8:10, New Living Translation)

Daddy's Little Girl

You'll always be your daddy's little girl,

Even when the passing years will take their toll,

More precious than the ruby or the pearl,

You are to me. Your love has touched my soul.

When you were born, I dropped down to one knee

And thanked God for this "blessing" in my life.

"Please guide her, God," I asked, "that she would be

A godly woman, intelligent and wise."

I long to see the time when you will grown

Into a beautiful woman of faith and love;

And that my little girl will come to know

The love of Christ, the "agape" from above.

When fathers, like winter blasts, have come and gone

Your Heavenly Father will lead and guide you on!

~~

Elder Howard J. Simon, Sr. and his wife, Addie, have four adult children and two grandchildren.

Reflections from Sharon's Heart

Life will never be completely perfect, but you can make the best of it!

"This is the day the Lord has made; We will rejoice and be glad in it." (Psalm 118:24, New King James Version).

You Make Me Proud

My Sweet Daughter,

I want you to understand that you were not the result of one night of passion. Instead, your mother and I furthered our mutual love for one another and through the grace of God you were conceived. As a matter of fact, I knew your mother was carrying you inside her before she even knew.

I often thought who would you look like, me or your mother and whose personality would you have and so forth. Those thoughts quickly faded because I realized the most important thing of all is that you were healthy. I loved you before we even met; I used to speak to you and speak life towards your purpose while you were still in your mother's womb.

Furthermore, I knew instantly you had purpose, I also knew that someday you'd stand before great people and astonish them not by speaking many elaborate words, but by your simple and profound wisdom and character, which is engraved with poise, grace and confidence.

Now that you are here and I can hold you in my arms, I quickly glance at your beauty, for you are far more beautiful than I could even imagine, but most importantly you're my baby girl. As I stare at you, I fall in love with your mother again and again. I can't stop kissing your big cheeks. I remember telling your mother she carried you for 9 months now it's my turn and I carried you everywhere we went.

Moreover, as I watched you grow from an infant to the young lady, I am so proud of you. Yet, there's one thing I understand and that is I place no demands on you as I know life can be cruel sometimes and it doesn't always seem to be easy to make the right decisions. So I won't add any further ridicule nor belittle your actions or decisions. Regardless of what decisions you make, I will forever love you. Your decisions will not make me love you any less. I just need you to bind this one thing to your heart, soul and memory and that is that *you must always believe in yourself and the gifts deposited within you because you were created to prosper and take others with you*!

With pride and eternal love.

~~

Minister Victor Mayon and his wife, Lisa, have two adult children and three grandchildren.

Reflections from Sharon's Heart

Your smile will light up a room and make others smile back at you.

"A cheerful heart is good medicine, but a broken spirit saps a person's strength" (Proverbs 17:22, New Living Translation).

Thank You

Let me start by giving Honor and Glory to GOD, THE FATHER, Who is the head of my life. I do this because He has everything to do with our emotions and feelings toward one another. Even more importantly, He is the author of our human purpose and structure for a sustained life form.

Believe me, this is not a science lesson in as much as it is a "life" lesson, but at some point, the two do relate. I'll explain. This magnificent body we have is equipped with feelings and emotions that cannot be changed by touch or arranged manually. Like the human spirit, it is changed only by our experiences and what we think of them. God instructs us to be fruitful and multiply. In other words, have children...have a family. In this, my story begins.

We grow up watching our parents (or parent) and we learn what is expected from us by watching them. The things that we learn are not always in line with the bible or even suitable for raising children. In some cases, having a child or raising a child is the last thing we think about when we embark on intimacy with the opposite sex. Emotions and feelings barely have a seat at the table. Being a product of a broken home, I can remember thinking, in anger, that once I had my own family, I'd never leave them and that I'd always be there to give guidance and love.

I was only 10 years old when I had these thoughts and I didn't know anything about companionship or marriage or how complicated both could be. I was all too eager to set forth on a path to learn about them. Let me be the first to say I should have been thinking about things that kids think about instead of how I can win someone's heart to make a family. I was entirely too young for that. The Simple 3 R's (reading, 'riting and 'rithmetic) could have filled that time just fine.

I failed miserably in my first marriage. I had been so preoccupied with my own wants that I forgot to pay close attention to my spouse. Needless to say, my family fell completely apart. I filled my head with thoughts of, "NEVER AGAIN". I'm thankful that God changed my mind and gave me wisdom when I met a darling young lady, whom I loved and cared about very much.

We dated and were a couple for two years and enjoyed each other's company immensely. Eventually, we were blessed with a beautiful baby girl who was the apple of my eye. It wasn't long before the flames of insecurity began again to burn and cause friction between my daughter's mom and me. This time when I left, I was sure that I was right for leaving. Again, I had lost the value of the meaning of family and what it offered:

1) I was no longer a mini-shepherd over the flock assigned to me.
2) Without a companion, I lacked a good reason to be reasonable or sensible.

3) I had no idea what my daughter's everyday struggles or joys were and I was not around to give her guidance through problems that she faced.

These things meant something to me, but I buried them behind things I saw outside the windmills of my own mind. I saw my daughter on occasion and the distance between grew wider and wider and I grew numb. I had almost come to the conclusion that I had no responsibility or purpose. I wasn't doing very well in life practices and I was having a hard time coming to grips with my perceived uselessness.

One day, I ran into my 5 year old daughter at a shopping mall, while she was with an older cousin. Her cousin knew me and respectfully greeted me. I reached for my daughter, with a huge smile on my face. She pulled away from me and grabbed tightly to her cousin's leg. I was crushed. It was at that moment that I knew that I had dropped the ball as a father. I had to ask for God's forgiveness.

The next couple of years were very tough because I was everywhere except where I wanted to be. I wanted to connect with my child and be responsible and share my life with her. Three years after that incident at the mall, my daughter's mother invited me to be a guest at our daughter's 6th grade graduation ceremony. I was elated to be connected with her and my daughter. My daughter's mother now had a young son and he and I bonded immediately.

This was the beginning of a great relationship for all of us, or so I thought. Still in the early stages of getting acquainted, my daughter was the most difficult to win over. Her mom and I were getting along fine and her little brother and I were unified through our love for sports. I had not made amends with my daughter yet, so her resentment was evident.

One day while we were out together as a family, my daughter was the only one who had money and her mother asked to borrow her money to purchase a meal for four, with the understanding that the money would be repaid upon returning home.

My daughter stated that she would buy a meal for her mom and for her brother, but in regards to me, she emphatically stated, "I'm not buying anything for him!" Stern words from her mom eventually convinced her to part with her money. My pride made me take small bites of the burger and I made up my mind to figure out a way to win her over. Making up my mind was not enough. I felt that the person I wanted to impress so much was not impressed with anything I did. The love that was given to me from heaven was rejecting me. Rejection is an emotion that we all handle badly. Men, women, boys and girls return to themselves to re-evaluate why they're rejected. I figured that I deserved what I got because I had dropped the ball earlier as a parent.

Months later, after a disagreement with her mom on an unrelated matter, I lost my temper and left the apartment, vowing never to return. I had begun walking and I was less than ¼ mile from our place when I heard footsteps quickly approaching me from behind. As I turned to check behind me, my daughter lunged forward to grab me around my waist and tightly hug me. She quietly said, "Don't leave." I could see the tears begin to well in her eyes and the look on her face told me that she desperately needed me to be the father that she needed. In that moment, I knew that I had to do my best to be there for my family.

Today, after 10 years of being absent from their lives, her mother (Saraya) and I have been married for more than 20 years. I've been there for the bumps and bruises, the joys, the laughter, the work projects, the proms, the first apartment and her wedding. Maraya, our daughter, now has two precious girls of her own. I don't even pretend to be the all-knowing man, because I've made more than my share of mistakes and wrong turns, but there's one thing I do know is that God blessed me when He returned a BLESSING OF LOVE back to me.

In closing, I'd like to say to men with daughters and to boys who will one day become men, men are commissioned to do God's work. To know what God's work is, we have to study HIS word so that we can go the right way. It's the only way to be a good example. Don't let your feelings of guilt for not being there keep you away from being the good in your child's life. They are a Gift from God and a steppingstone for your future.

Lay your path straight so that your children will know the way to go.

God bless you.

~~

Mahlon Potts and his wife, Saraya, have two adult children and two grandchildren.

Reflections from Sharon's Heart

Attitude is everything, so do your best to have a good attitude at all times.

Therefore, if anyone is in Christ, he is a new creation. The old has passed away; behold, the new has come (2 Corinthians 5:17, English Standard Version).

What would you say to inspire yourself or others?

_____

_____

_____

_____

_____

_____

_____

Final Thoughts

It is our hope that this book has encouraged you! One thing is sure: we all need and want to be loved. It doesn't matter how young or old someone is, feeling loved can be great motivation! If you don't feel loved, LOVE YOURSELF!

Life is a beautiful gift, so find what makes you happy and pursue that with all your might.

Remind yourself that you are beautiful and worthy of love.

More inspiration!

Say yes to new adventures.

It is better to be yourself and have no friends than to lose yourself by trying to fit in.

Stop doubting yourself.

The difference between winning and losing is not quitting.

Even when it seems like your life is falling apart, don't lose hope.

Believe in yourself and you can do unbelievable things.

Do what others think you can't do.

Set goals that make you want to jump out of bed each day.

Thank You!

Thank you for purchasing this book. Your support warms my heart.

Show genuine kindness to a young lady and show that you care and watch her soar!

Resources for Teen Girls

Check out these organizations that will keep you motivated to keep moving forward and upward!

Positive Results Corporation
http://www.prc123.org/

Life Lifters International
http://lifeliftersinternational.org/

Miss Greater West Coast
http://www.missgwc.com/

LeaderHERShip Academy
www.LeaderHERshipAcademy.org

Boys and Girls Club of America
https://www.bgca.org/

Let's Stay Connected!

Email: Sharon_Judie@yahoo.com
Facebook: 10TalentsProductions
Instagram: SharonYJudie
Twitter: SharonJudie1

About the Author

Sharon Y. Judie lives in Southern California with her husband, Carl. She is a playwright, producer and director. *Heart to Heart: Encouragement, Advice and Inspiration for Teen Girls* is her first book.

www.ingramcontent.com/pod-product-compliance
Lightning Source LLC
Chambersburg PA
CBHW072022040426
42447CB00009B/1690